Cookies

Favorite Recipes for a Classic Treat

D1404839

BARNES & NOBLE

Introduction

Of all the sweet snacks concocted in our kitchens, there is none more versatile than the cookie—recipes range from kid-in-the-kitchen simple to traditional gourmet to a bold baker's creative masterpiece. Amazingly versatile, cookies come in an abundance of different tastes and textures. Butter, sugar, nuts, chocolate, espresso, candies, fruits, jams, jellies, and peanut butter are just a few of the countless ingredients that have found their way into the mixing bowl. Adjustable to any hand size, cookies can be eaten on the run or, in a more formal setting, on plates accompanied by cups of tea or coffee. Cookies are at home in a variety of settings—in decorative jars, picnic baskets, packed in brown bags with sandwiches, or hanging on Christmas trees. They are suitable for any occasion and can fit any bill of fare.

Baking cookies that look as wonderful as they taste requires organization more than skill, for with a little practice, skill can be acquired. To help facilitate your baking pursuits, this book is divided into sections, clearly marked with tabs, for each method of preparation or type of cookie: Rolled Cookies, Drop Cookies, Sliced Cookies, Hand-shaped Cookies, and Bar Cookies, plus a special section called Favorites, for recipes that have proven appeal for friends and family. Each section offers a number of easy-to-follow recipes for every occasion, as well as fill-in pages so you can record your own favorite recipes as well as new ones given to you by friends.

The cookie cutters included in this kit are perfect for the rolled cookies featured here, like Judie's Wine Stars and Valentine Hearts. Before turning to a section and beginning to assemble your ingredients, be sure to read the introductory recipes for vanilla and chocolate sables and the basic icings—all are essential blueprints for your cookie-baking ventures, and many of the recipes featured in this book refer to them.

From Stained Glass Windows to Chocolate Checkerboards to Raspberry Coconut Bars, there's something for every connoisseur of sweets within these pages. With the easy-to-follow recipes, helpful baking tips, and stainless steel cutters contained in this wonderful kit, even novice bakers can yield gourmet results.

Tips for Better Baking

❋ When baking, always measure ingredients carefully, using appropriate liquid and dry standard measuring spoons and cups.

❋ Shiny baking pans and cookie sheets are best–they reflect heat well, resulting in beautiful golden crusts. If you are using a pan with a dark, nonstick surface, reduce the oven temperature 25°F.

❋ Be sure to allow time for your oven to preheat–an oven takes 10 to 15 minutes to reach 350°F.

❋ Purchase baking powder in small quantities, as it loses its effectiveness over time. To test if baking powder is fresh, mix a teaspoon into a quarter cup of very hot water. If the mixture fizzes vigorously, the baking powder is still good.

❋ Don't crowd pans in the oven. They should not touch each other or the sides of the oven, and shouldn't be set above or below other pans on the rack.

❋ Be careful if you are substituting a low-fat spread for butter, margarine, or shortening in a recipe. Fat is essential to the baking process, and the recipe may not turn out as well as it might have using the original ingredient. Special low-fat recipes take into account the effects of reduced–fat ingredients.

Essential Equipment for Making Decorated Cookies

Baking sheets
Cookie cutters
Fine paintbrush
Medium–size writing tip
Metal spatula
Nonstick cooking spray

Paper piping bag
Pastry brush
Rolling pin
Sharp knife
Wax paper or plastic wrap
Wire cooling racks

Mastering these basic recipes is essential to making many of the delicious, beautifully decorated cookies featured in this book.

Vanilla Sables

Makes about 20 cookies

2^1/$_4$ cups flour
^{7}/$_8$ cup firm unsalted butter
^{3}/$_4$ cup confectioners' sugar

2 egg yolks
1 teaspoon vanilla extract

1. Preheat the oven to 400°F and grease two baking sheets.

2. Put the flour in a food processor. Cut the butter into small pieces, add it to the food processor and pulse until the mixture resembles breadcrumbs. Or, put the flour and butter in a medium mixing bowl and, with a pastry blender or two knives, cut the butter into the flour until the mixture is crumbly. Add the sugar, egg yolks, and vanilla extract and blend into a smooth dough. Wrap in wax paper or plastic wrap and refrigerate for 1 hour.

3. Roll out the dough on a floured surface, cut out rounds or squares, and place them on the baking sheets. Bake for 6 to 10 minutes, or until the cookies turn golden around the edges. Remove the cookies to wire racks to cool completely.

Chocolate Sables

Makes about 20 cookies

2 cups flour
^{1}/$_4$ cup cocoa powder
^{7}/$_8$ cup firm unsalted butter

^{3}/$_4$ cup confectioners' sugar
2 egg yolks
1 teaspoon vanilla extract

1. Preheat the oven to 400°F and grease two baking sheets.

2. Put the flour and cocoa powder in a food processor. Cut the butter into small pieces, add it to the food processor and pulse until the mixture resembles breadcrumbs. Or, put the flour–cocoa mixture and butter in a medium mixing bowl and, with a pastry blender or two knives, cut the butter into the flour until the

mixture is crumbly. Add the sugar, egg yolks, and vanilla extract and blend into a smooth dough. Wrap in wax paper or plastic wrap and refrigerate for 1 hour.

3. Roll out the dough on a floured surface, cut out rounds or squares, and place them on the baking sheets. Bake for 6 to 10 minutes, or until the cookies turn golden around the edges. Remove the cookies to wire racks to cool completely.

Glaze

Makes a single quantity

1 egg white
1 tablespoon lemon juice

$1^{1}/_{4}$ cups confectioners' sugar, sifted

1. In a small bowl, lightly whisk the egg white and lemon juice.

2. Gradually whisk in the confectioners' sugar until the mixture is smooth and has the consistency of cream.

3. Cover the surface of the glaze with plastic wrap to prevent a crust from forming until ready for use.

Royal Icing

Makes a single quantity

1 egg white

$1^{3}/_{4}$ cups confectioners' sugar, sifted

1. In a small bowl, lightly whisk the egg white. Gradually whisk in confectioners' sugar until the icing is thick enough to form soft peaks.

2. Cover the surface of the icing with plastic wrap to prevent a crust from forming until ready for use.

From *Decorating Cookies* by Joanna Farrow. Copyright ©2000 Merehurst Limited, First published in the United States of America in 2001 by Watson–Guptill Publications, New York. www.watsonguptill.com

Valentine Hearts

Lace Snowflakes

Valentine Hearts

These pretty hearts make ideal gifts or decorations for Valentine, engagement, wedding, or anniversary celebrations.

Makes 16 to 18 hearts

Special equipment:
3-inch and $1/2$-inch heart–shaped cookie cutters
drinking straw to make holes, if desired
narrow ribbon, if desired

Vanilla Sable dough (see introduction)

Icing and decoration:
a single quantity Glaze (see introduction)
$1^3/4$ ounces store-bought rolled fondant
confectioners' sugar for dusting
a single quantity Royal Icing (see introduction)
silver dragees

1. Preheat the oven to 400°F and grease two baking sheets. Roll out the vanilla sable dough on a floured surface and use the large cutter to cut out hearts. Transfer them to the baking sheets and bake for 8 minutes, or until golden around the edges. Leave on the baking sheets for 2 minutes, then transfer them to wire racks to cool.

2. Using a palette knife or narrow metal spatula, spread the glaze over the hearts in a thin, even layer, just to the edges of the hearts.

3. On a surface dusted with confectioners' sugar, roll the fondant to about $1/8$ inch thickness. Using the small cookie cutter, cut out heart shapes from the fondant.

4. Put the royal icing in a piping bag fitted with a medium writing tip. Pipe a small amount of icing onto the center of about half of the large heart cookies. Position the fondant hearts over the icing and gently push them in place. Allow to dry for 30 minutes.

5. Use the small cutter to impress heart shapes into the icing on the remaining cookies. Leave about $1/4$ inch between each heart and vary the angles of each.

6. Pipe a border around the edge of each cookie, then pipe borders around the edges of the smaller heart cookies and press a dragee into the icing at the top of each. Pipe decorative wavy filigree lines all over the glaze (see photograph on divider).

7. On the remaining cookies, pipe over the heart-shaped impressions to accentuate the heart shapes, and secure dragees at intervals between the hearts, securing each with a dot of icing.

TIP

If you want to hang the cookies or tie them to gifts, before baking, use a drinking straw to make holes near the tops of the hearts so that they can be threaded with ribbons.

From *Decorating Cookies* by Joanna Farrow. Copyright ©2000 Merehurst Limited, First published in the United States of America in 2001 by Watson-Guptill Publications, New York. www.watsonguptill.com

Lace Snowflakes

With their attractive piped snowflake centers, you will be tempted to keep these stars hanging on the Christmas tree throughout the festive season.

Makes 14 snowflakes

Special equipment:
$4^1/_2$-inch and $2^1/_2$-inch 6-point star cutters
narrow white or silver ribbon

Vanilla Sable dough (see introduction)

Icing and decoration:
a single quantity Glaze (see introduction)
edible white glitter
a single quantity royal icing (see introduction)

1. Preheat the oven to 400°F. Lightly grease two baking sheets. Roll out the vanilla sable dough on a floured surface and cut out star shapes using the large star cutter. Reroll the trimmings as necessary to make 14 cookies. Transfer the star shapes to the baking sheets.

2. Using the small star cutter, cut out the center of each star. If the cutter starts to stick to the dough, clean it and dust with a little flour. Bake for 6 to 7 minutes, or until the cookies turn golden around the edges. Leave the cookies on the baking sheet for 2 minutes, then carefully transfer them to a wire cooling rack.

3. Place a tray or sheet of wax paper under the rack. Using a pastry brush, coat the tops of the stars with the glaze. Brush any glaze away from the inner points with a toothpick. Repeat until all the cookies are iced. Leave to dry for 1 hour.

4. Brush the stars very lightly with a clean, barely damp pastry brush and sprinkle them with edible glitter. Be careful not to wet the glaze or it will dissolve.

5. Lift the cookies off the rack and lay them on a sheet of clean wax paper. Shave off any drips of icing from the undersides of the stars if they are not sitting flat on the paper.

6. Put royal icing in a piping bag fitted with a medium writing tip. Pipe three lines across each star from the inner points of the star so that they cross in the center. Pipe snowflake designs over the crossed lines (see photograph on divider). Leave to set overnight.

7. Carefully peel the paper away and use lengths of ribbon (strung through the center of each cookie) to hang the snowflakes from the tree.

From *Decorating Cookies* by Joanna Farrow. Copyright ©2000 Merehurst Limited, First published in the United States of America in 2001 by Watson–Guptill Publications, New York. www.watsonguptill.com

Stained Glass Windows

Clear candies melted into different shapes give these tantalizing cookies the look of stained glass.

Makes about 5 dozen cookies

Special equipment:
a variety of both small and
 large cookie cutters
sharp paring knife
drinking straw to make holes
 for hanging, if desired
narrow ribbon, if desired

1^1/$_3$ cups butter
1^1/$_3$ cups sugar
^{1}/$_2$ cup milk
4 eggs
1^1/$_4$ teaspoons nutmeg
5^1/$_4$ cups flour
clear hard candies, sorted by
 color and crushed

1. In a large mixing bowl, cream the butter and sugar. In a small mixing bowl, mix the milk and eggs, then beat into the butter mixture. Add the nutmeg to the flour, and then gradually mix into the butter mixture. Wrap in wax paper or plastic wrap and refrigerate for 1 hour.

2. Preheat oven to 350°F. Cover two baking sheets with foil. Lightly spray foil with cooking spray.

3. Roll dough ^{1}/$_4$ inch thick and cut out with large cookie cutters of your choice. From the center of each cookie, cut out a smaller shape using a smaller cookie cutter or a paring knife, making sure to leave at least ^{1}/$_4$ inch of edge around the center hole. Carefully place the cookies on prepared baking sheets.

4. Fill open centers with crushed candy, one color to a hole. If you are planning to use the cookies as ornaments, use a drinking straw to cut a hole through the top of each cookie (through which you'll be able to pass a ribbon).

5. Bake 6 to 9 minutes, or until the candy melts. Cool 5 minutes to solidify candy before carefully moving the cookies to wire racks to cool completely.

Judie's Wine Stars

A touch of sherry or port makes this a perfect cookie for the grown-ups on your list.

Makes 4 to 5 dozen cookies

$1/2$ cup unsalted butter, at
  room temperature
$1^1/_2$ cups light brown sugar,
  packed
1 large egg
$1/2$ cup finely chopped
  blanched almonds

3 tablespoons sherry or port
$1/_8$ teaspoon almond extract
$2^1/_2$ cups flour
$3/_4$ teaspoon cinnamon
$1/_2$ teaspoon baking soda

1. Preheat oven to 400°F. Lightly spray two baking sheets with cooking spray.

2. In a large mixing bowl, cream the butter and sugar together until light and fluffy. Beat in the egg, almonds, sherry or port, and almond extract.

3. In a small bowl, stir together the flour, cinnamon, and baking soda and add to the butter mixture. Mix until well combined.

4. On a well-floured surface, roll out the dough to $1/4$ inch thickness. Cut out stars and place 1 inch apart on prepared baking sheets. Bake 10 to 12 minutes, or until cookies are lightly browned.

Gingerbread Folk

Gather the children to help make and decorate these traditionally spiced Christmas favorites.

Makes about 4 dozen cookies

Special equipment:
people–shaped cookie cutter(s)

$^1/_2$ cup butter or margarine, softened
1 cup light brown sugar, packed
$1^1/_2$ cups light molasses
$^2/_3$ cup water
$6^1/_2$ cups flour
2 teaspoons baking soda
2 teaspoons salt

2 teaspoons ground ginger
1 teaspoon ground cinnamon
1 teaspoon ground allspice
$^1/_2$ teaspoon ground cloves

Icing and decoration:
raisins, semisweet chocolate pieces, colored sprinkles, sugar, and/or nuts
2 cups sifted confectioners' sugar
2 to 3 tablespoons milk or light cream

1. In a large bowl, beat butter or margarine and sugar until creamy. Add the molasses and beat until blended, then mix in the water. In another large bowl, stir together flour, baking soda, salt, ginger, cinnamon, allspice, and cloves. Gradually beat dry mixture into butter mixture until dough is stiff and well blended. Divide the dough into quarters. Wrap in plastic wrap and refrigerate for at least 4 hours.

2. Preheat the oven to 350°F. Lightly grease two baking sheets.

3. Roll dough $^1/_4$ inch thick. Cut out cookies with people–shaped cookie cutters. Transfer to baking sheets. Press raisins, chocolate pieces, sprinkles, sugar, and/or nuts into place before baking.

4. Bake 10 to 12 minutes, or until lightly browned. Remove cookies to wire racks to cool completely.

5. Once the cookies are cool, mix together the confectioners' sugar and 2 to 3 tablespoons of milk or light cream to make a thick icing. With a piping bag and small writing tip, outline the shapes and make eyes, noses, and smiles. Let the pieces set for 2 to 3 hours before storing in airtight containers.

Cinnamon Stars

These spicy butter cookies will simply melt in your mouth.

Makes 5 to 10 dozen cookies, depending on size

Special equipment:
1- or 2-inch star-shaped
   cookie cutter

1¹/₄ cups butter, softened
³/₄ cup confectioners' sugar

2¹/₂ cups flour
2 teaspoons cinnamon
¹/₂ teaspoon nutmeg
1 teaspoon vanilla
Confectioners' sugar for
   sprinkling

1. In a large bowl, cream the butter. Gradually add ³/₄ cup confectioners' sugar, beating until light and fluffy. In a small bowl, stir together flour, cinnamon, and nutmeg. Add the dry ingredients to the creamed mixture. Stir in the vanilla and mix well. Divide into four equal portions. Wrap with wax paper or plastic wrap and chill 1 hour.

2. Preheat oven to 325°F. Do not grease baking sheets.

3. On a lightly floured surface, roll out one portion of the dough at a time, to a thickness of ¹/₄ inch. Cut out with a 1- or 2-inch star-shaped cookie cutter, dipping the cutter in flour as needed to keep dough from sticking.

4. Place cookies on ungreased baking sheets and bake 12 to 15 minutes for 1-inch cookies, 15 to 18 minutes for 2-inch cookies. Remove to wire racks to cool. Sprinkle cookies with confectioners' sugar.

✤ RECIPE:

✤ From the kitchen of:

✤ Yield: _____   ✤ Preheat oven: _____

✤ Ingredients: _____

✤ Directions: _____

✤ Special notes: _____

❋ RECIPE: _____

❋ From the kitchen of: _____

❋ Yield: _____   ❋ Preheat oven: _____

❋ Ingredients: _____   _____

_____   _____

_____   _____

_____   _____

_____   _____

_____   _____

❋ Directions: _____

_____

_____

_____

_____

_____

_____

_____

_____

_____

_____

_____

_____

_____

❋ Special notes: _____

_____

_____

_____

✽ RECIPE:

✽ From the kitchen of: _____

✽ Yield: _____   ✽ Preheat oven: _____

✽ Ingredients: _____

_____   _____

_____   _____

_____   _____

_____   _____

✽ Directions: _____

_____

_____

_____

_____

_____

_____

_____

_____

_____

_____

_____

✽ Special notes: _____

_____

_____

✳ RECIPE:

✳ From the kitchen of:

✳ Yield: _____ ✳ Preheat oven: _____

✳ Ingredients:

✳ Directions:

✳ Special notes:

✳ RECIPE: _____

✳ From the kitchen of: _____

✳ Yield: _____   ✳ Preheat oven: _____

✳ Ingredients: _____   _____

_____   _____

_____   _____

_____   _____

_____   _____

✳ Directions: _____

_____

_____

_____

_____

_____

_____

_____

_____

_____

_____

_____

_____

✳ Special notes: _____

_____

_____

�֎ RECIPE:

✤ From the kitchen of: _____

✤ Yield: _____   ✤ Preheat oven: _____

✤ Ingredients: _____   _____

_____   _____

_____   _____

_____   _____

_____   _____

_____

✤ Directions: _____

_____

_____

_____

_____

_____

_____

_____

_____

_____

_____

_____

_____

_____

✤ Special notes: _____

_____

_____

_____

Pumpkin Drop Cookies

Oatmeal Raisin Cookies

Chocolate Chunk Macadamia Nut Cookies

Especially Chocolate Cookies

Pumpkin Drop Cookies

Even your favorite "cookie monster" will love
these delicious, nutritious cookies.

Makes 4 dozen cookies

1 cup sugar
$^1/_2$ cup butter or margarine
1 egg
1 cup canned pumpkin
1 teaspoon vanilla
2 cups flour
1 teaspoon baking soda
$^3/_4$ teaspoon cinnamon
$^1/_4$ teaspoon salt
$^1/_4$ teaspoon nutmeg
1 cup raisins

1 cup chopped pecans or
  walnuts

Frosting:
2 cups confectioners' sugar
2 tablespoons butter or
  margarine, softened
3 tablespoons finely shredded
  orange peel
2 tablespoons orange juice

1. Preheat oven to 375°F. Lightly grease two baking sheets.

2. In a large bowl, cream together sugar and butter or margarine
until light and fluffy. Add egg, pumpkin, and vanilla; mix well.

3. In a medium bowl, stir together flour, baking soda, cinnamon,
salt, and nutmeg. Add gradually to the pumpkin mixture, stirring
until blended. With a large spoon, fold in raisins and nuts.

4. Drop dough by rounded teaspoonfuls onto the baking sheets.
Bake 12 to 15 minutes, or until lightly browned. Remove to wire
racks to cool completely.

5. In a small bowl, cream the confectioners' sugar, butter, 2 tablespoons of the orange peel, and the orange juice. Spread the frosting
on the cookies. Garnish with reserved orange peel.

Oatmeal Raisin Cookies

These big, soft cookies are even better when served with glasses of ice-cold milk.

Makes 1½ to 2 dozen large cookies

1 cup butter or margarine, at
  room temperature
1 cup sugar
2 eggs
1 teaspoon vanilla
2 cups flour
1 teaspoon baking powder

1 teaspoon baking soda
½ teaspoon salt
½ cup milk
2 cups uncooked oatmeal
1½ cups raisins
1½ cups walnut pieces,
  optional

1. Preheat oven to 375°F. Lightly grease two baking sheets.

2. In a large mixing bowl, cream the butter or margarine and sugar until light and fluffy. Mix in the eggs and vanilla. In a small mixing bowl, stir together the flour, baking powder, baking soda, and salt. Add half the dry ingredients to the butter mixture; add the milk, then add the remaining dry ingredients and stir to combine. Fold in the oatmeal, raisins, and walnuts.

3. Spoon heaping tablespoons 2 inches apart onto prepared baking sheets. Bake 12 to 15 minutes, or until cookies are lightly browned. Remove cookies to wire racks to cool.

VARIATION: Add 1 cup peanut butter chips to the batter.

Chocolate Chunk
Macadamia Nut Cookies

Rich, chewy cookies bursting with nuts and chunks of chocolate
are an appreciated treat any time of year.

Makes 1¹/₂ to 2 dozen cookies

³/₄ cup granulated sugar
³/₄ cup light brown sugar,
  packed
¹/₂ cup unsalted butter, at
  room temperature
¹/₂ cup shortening

1 egg
2 teaspoons vanilla
2¹/₂ cups flour
1 teaspoon baking soda
1¹/₄ cups chocolate chunks
³/₄ cup macadamia nuts, halved

1. Preheat oven to 375°F. Do not grease baking sheets.

2. In a large mixing bowl, cream the granulated sugar and the
brown sugar, butter, and shortening until light and fluffy. Beat in
the egg and vanilla. Add the flour and baking soda; mix thoroughly. Fold in chocolate chunks and macadamia nuts and blend
until thoroughly mixed.

3. Drop by large rounded tablespoons 3 inches apart on ungreased
baking sheets. Lightly press cookies with the bottom of a drinking
glass to flatten slightly, and bake 10 to 12 minutes, or until lightly
browned. Remove cookies to wire racks to cool.

Especially Chocolate Cookies

These are perfect treats for a chocoholic friend. Almonds and raspberry-flavored chocolate chips complement the chocolate and punch up the flavor.

Makes 2 to 2 1/2 dozen very large cookies

1½ cups granulated sugar
1½ cups dark brown sugar, packed
1 cup unsalted butter, at room temperature
2 eggs
1 teaspoon vanilla
2 ounces unsweetened chocolate, melted and cooled to room temperature

2½ cups flour
¼ cup unsweetened cocoa
1 teaspoon baking soda
½ teaspoon salt
1 cup chocolate chunks
1 cup raspberry-flavored chocolate chips
1 cup slivered almonds

1. Preheat oven to 375°F. Lightly spray two baking sheets with cooking spray.

2. In a large bowl, cream the granulated sugar and the brown sugar with the butter until light and fluffy. Add the eggs, vanilla, and melted chocolate; beat well. In a small bowl, stir together the flour, cocoa, baking soda, and salt and add half at a time to the creamed mixture, blending thoroughly. Fold in the chocolate chunks, chips, and almonds.

3. Place heaping tablespoonfuls of dough 3 inches apart on the prepared baking sheets. Bake 12 to 14 minutes. Let the cookies remain on the baking sheets for 5 minutes, then remove to wire racks to cool completely.

✳ RECIPE: _____

✳ From the kitchen of: _____

✳ Yield: _____   ✳ Preheat oven: _____

✳ Ingredients: _____   _____

_____   _____

_____   _____

_____   _____

_____   _____

✳ Directions: _____

_____

_____

_____

_____

_____

_____

_____

_____

_____

_____

_____

✳ Special notes: _____

_____

_____

_____

✳ RECIPE: _____

✳ From the kitchen of: _____

✳ Yield: _____   ✳ Preheat oven: _____

✳ Ingredients: _____   _____

_____   _____

_____   _____

_____   _____

_____   _____

_____   _____

✳ Directions: _____

_____

_____

_____

_____

_____

_____

_____

_____

_____

_____

_____

_____

_____

✳ Special notes: _____

_____

_____

_____

✤ RECIPE: _____

✤ From the kitchen of: _____

✤ Yield: _____   ✤ Preheat oven: _____

✤ Ingredients: _____   _____

_____   _____

_____   _____

_____   _____

_____   _____

_____   _____

✤ Directions: _____

_____

_____

_____

_____

_____

_____

_____

_____

_____

_____

_____

_____

_____

_____

✤ Special notes: _____

_____

_____

_____

✳ RECIPE:

✳ From the kitchen of:

✳ Yield: _____   ✳ Preheat oven: _____

✳ Ingredients:

✳ Directions:

✳ Special notes:

✽ RECIPE: _____

✽ From the kitchen of: _____

✽ Yield: _____   ✽ Preheat oven: _____

✽ Ingredients: _____   _____

_____   _____

_____   _____

_____   _____

_____   _____

_____   _____

✽ Directions: _____

_____

_____

_____

_____

_____

_____

_____

_____

_____

_____

_____

_____

_____

_____

_____

_____

✽ Special notes: _____

_____

_____

_____

❋ RECIPE: _____

❋ From the kitchen of: _____

❋ Yield: _____   ❋ Preheat oven: _____

❋ Ingredients: _____

_____   _____

_____   _____

_____   _____

_____   _____

_____   _____

❋ Directions: _____

_____

_____

_____

_____

_____

_____

_____

_____

_____

_____

_____

_____

_____

❋ Special notes: _____

_____

_____

_____

Chocolate Checkerboards

Almond Slices

Simple ingredients are the secret behind this delicious cookie.
The dough can be made well in advance, then sliced and baked
whenever you want to enjoy fresh, warm cookies.

Makes about 4 dozen cookies

1 cup unsalted butter, at
   room temperature
$^1/_2$ cup granulated sugar
$^1/_2$ cup light brown sugar,
   packed
1 egg

1 teaspoon vanilla
$^3/_4$ teaspoon almond extract
$2^1/_2$ cups flour
1 teaspoon baking soda
$^1/_2$ teaspoon cinnamon
1 cup slivered almonds, toasted

1. In a large mixing bowl, cream butter, granulated sugar, and
brown sugar until light and fluffy; add the egg, vanilla, and
almond extract. Mix in the flour, baking soda, and cinnamon.
Fold in the almonds.

2. Divide the dough in half, placing each half on a sheet of wax
paper. Flour your hands and shape each piece into a roll approximately 10 inches long and 2 inches in diameter. Wrap each roll in
wax paper, twisting ends of the paper, and refrigerate overnight.

3. Preheat oven to 375°F. Lightly spray two baking sheets with
cooking spray.

4. Remove rolls from the refrigerator, unwrap, and cut into $^1/_4$-inch
slices. Place the slices 1 inch apart on prepared baking sheets and
bake 12 to 14 minutes, or until lightly browned. Remove cookies
to wire racks to cool.

Galettes

These wonderfully rich butter cookies are an adaptation of
those found in the Brittany.

Makes 4 to 5 dozen cookies

2 cups unsalted butter, at room
temperature
1 cup granulated sugar
1 teaspoon vanilla
$^1/_2$ teaspoon almond extract

3 cups flour
1 teaspoon baking powder
4 tablespoons butter, melted
turbinado sugar, for sprinkling

1. In a large bowl, cream the butter and sugar until light and
fluffy. Beat in the vanilla and almond extract. Mix in the flour
and baking powder until well combined.

2. Lay a sheet of wax paper on a smooth surface. Spoon half the
sticky dough onto wax paper. Lightly flour your hands and form a
roll approximately 9 inches long and 2 inches in diameter. Repeat
with remaining dough. Wrap each roll in wax paper, twisting ends
of the paper, and refrigerate 3 hours.

3. Preheat oven to 400°F. Do not grease baking sheets.

4. Take dough out of the refrigerator, unwrap, and cut into $^1/_4$–inch
slices. Place slices 2 inches apart on ungreased baking sheets. Using
a pastry brush, lightly coat top of each cookie with melted butter
and sprinkle with the turbinado sugar. Bake 12 to 14 minutes, or
until cookies are nicely browned. Remove cookies to wire racks
to cool.

Peanut Butter & Chocolate Swirls

Placed in the center of each swirl, "Red Hots" —cinnamon-flavored candies— provide an unusual taste dimension. You can find these fiery red buttons in grocery, candy, and large drug stores.

Makes 3 to 4 dozen cookies

Peanut butter dough:
1/2 cup unsalted butter, at
   room temperature
1/2 cup creamy peanut butter
1/2 cup dark brown sugar,
   packed
1 teaspoon vanilla
1 1/2 cups flour
1 1/2 teaspoons baking powder

Chocolate dough:
1/2 cup unsalted butter, at
   room temperature

1/2 cup granulated sugar
1 egg yolk
2 ounces unsweetened chocolate,
   melted and cooled to room
   temperature
1/2 teaspoon vanilla
1 1/2 cups flour
1/4 cup unsweetened cocoa
1 1/2 teaspoons baking powder

Decoration:
1 box of Red Hots

1. For the peanut butter dough: in a large mixing bowl, cream the butter, peanut butter, and sugar until light and fluffy. Blend in the vanilla. In a small bowl, stir together the flour and baking powder and add to the creamed butter mixture, mixing until a dough forms. Wrap dough in wax paper or plastic wrap. Chill for at least 1 hour but not more than 2 hours.

2. For the chocolate dough: in a large mixing bowl, cream the butter and sugar until light and fluffy. Beat in the egg yolk, chocolate, and vanilla. In a small bowl, stir together the flour, cocoa, and baking powder and add to the creamed butter mixture, mixing until a dough forms. Wrap dough in wax paper or plastic wrap. Chill for at least 1 hour but not more than 2 hours.

3. Unwrap both doughs and divide each in half. Place half the chocolate dough on a sheet of floured wax paper and gently roll into a 12-by-7-inch rectangle. Leave the dough on the wax paper

and set aside. Using a fresh sheet of wax paper, repeat with half the peanut butter dough.

4. Carefully flip the chocolate rectangle on top of the peanut butter rectangle. Using the wax paper to lift the dough, roll the 12-inch length into a tight tube. Repeat this process with the remaining dough. Wrap in fresh wax paper or plastic wrap and chill overnight.

5. Preheat oven to 375°F. Lightly grease two baking sheets.

6. Unwrap the rolls and cut into $1/2$-inch slices. Place the slices 1 inch apart on baking sheets and place a Red Hot in the center of each cookie. Bake 12 to 15 minutes, or until the cookies are lightly browned. Remove cookies from the oven and allow them to remain on baking sheet for 5 minutes, then remove them to wire racks to cool.

Chocolate Checkerboards

These buttery, two-tone squares are easy to shape and the contrast is extremely effective. Melted chocolate adds a perfect finishing touch.

Makes about 5 dozen cookies

Special equipment:
2 plastic sandwich bags

Vanilla Sable dough (see introduction)
Chocolate Sable dough (see introduction)
small amount of beaten egg white

small amount of flour

Icing and decoration:
$2^1/_2$ ounces semisweet chocolate
$2^1/_2$ ounces white chocolate

1. Preheat the oven to 400°F. Lightly grease a large baking sheet. On a lightly floured sheet of wax paper, roll out the vanilla sable dough to a 12-by-$4^1/_2$-inch rectangle, about $^5/_8$ inch thick. Keep the dough in a neat block as you work, so that very little of the dough will need to be trimmed off once the checkerboard pattern is shaped (see photograph on divider). Repeat with the chocolate mixture.

2. To help the two doughs adhere, brush the vanilla dough with a small amount of beaten egg white. Pick up the wax paper under the chocolate dough and flip the chocolate dough onto the vanilla dough, then peel off the wax paper.

3. With a sharp, lightly floured knife, cut the rectangle of stacked dough in half, lengthwise. Brush one of the halves with egg white and then, lining up the cut edges, stack the other half on top so the colors alternate. Carefully trim off the uncut edges of the dough.

4. Use the lightly floured knife to cut the dough block lengthwise into four evenly sized strips. Re-flour the knife after each cut.

5. Brushing each layer with egg white to secure them, reassemble the stack so that the colors alternate, creating a checkerboard design.

6. Slice the stack widthwise into $1/4$-inch slices and transfer the pieces to the baking sheet, spacing them 1 inch apart. Bake for 12 to 15 minutes, or until the squares just begin to darken around the edges. Leave on the baking sheet for 2 minutes before transferring to wire racks to cool.

7. Break the plain and white chocolate into pieces in separate bowls, and melt in a double boiler. Put each type of melted chocolate into plastic sandwich bags and, with scissors, snip off a tiny corner from each bag. Use the semisweet chocolate to pipe decorative dots and lines on half the cookies. Use the white chocolate to pipe decorations over the remaining cookies.

8. Set in a cool place for 2 hours before transferring the cookies to an airtight container.

TIP

Shaping these checkerboards is easier when the dough is well chilled.

From *Decorating Cookies* by Joanna Farrow. Copyright ©2000 Merehurst Limited, First published in the United States of America in 2001 by Watson–Guptill Publications, New York. www.watsonguptill.com

✤ RECIPE:

✤ From the kitchen of: _____

✤ Yield: _____   ✤ Preheat oven: _____

✤ Ingredients: _____

_____   _____

_____   _____

_____   _____

_____   _____

_____   _____

✤ Directions: _____

_____

_____

_____

_____

_____

_____

_____

_____

_____

_____

_____

_____

_____

_____

_____

✤ Special notes: _____

_____

_____

_____

❋ RECIPE:

❋ From the kitchen of:

❋ Yield: _____   ❋ Preheat oven: _____

❋ Ingredients: _____

❋ Directions:

❋ Special notes:

✣ RECIPE:

✣ From the kitchen of:

✣ Yield: _____   ✣ Preheat oven: _____

✣ Ingredients:

✣ Directions:

✣ Special notes:

✳ RECIPE: _____

✳ From the kitchen of: _____

✳ Yield: _____   ✳ Preheat oven: _____

✳ Ingredients: _____   _____

_____   _____

_____   _____

_____   _____

_____   _____

✳ Directions: _____

_____

_____

_____

_____

_____

_____

_____

_____

_____

_____

_____

_____

_____

✳ Special notes: _____

_____

_____

_____

✢ RECIPE:

✢ From the kitchen of: _____

✢ Yield: _____   ✢ Preheat oven: _____

✢ Ingredients: _____

✢ Directions: _____

✢ Special notes: _____

✳ RECIPE: _____

✳ From the kitchen of: _____

✳ Yield: _____ ✳ Preheat oven: _____

✳ Ingredients: _____

_____ _____

_____ _____

_____ _____

_____ _____

_____ _____

✳ Directions: _____

_____

_____

_____

_____

_____

_____

_____

_____

_____

_____

_____

_____

_____

✳ Special notes: _____

_____

_____

_____

Elizabeth Newkirk's Coconut Macaroons

Black and White "Pretzels"

Pecan Crescents

Mexican Chocolate Sugar Cookies

Elizabeth Newkirk's Coconut Macaroons

Macaroons are flourless cookies traditionally served in Jewish homes during Passover. Their festive look and timeless sweet flavor make them a great cookie for any holiday, any time of year.

Makes approximately 1½ to 2 dozen cookies

2⅔ cups flaked coconut, packed
1 cup sweetened condensed milk
2 teaspoons vanilla

¾ teaspoon almond extract
¼ teaspoon salt

1. Preheat oven to 350°F. Heavily grease two baking sheets with shortening.

2. Combine all ingredients in a medium mixing bowl, blending until the coconut is wet and the condensed milk is completely absorbed.

3. Spoon rounded teaspoonfuls onto baking sheets, 1½ inches apart. With your fingers, shape cookies into mounds.

4. Bake 10 to 12 minutes, or until browned on the bottom and slightly brown on top. Let cookies remain on baking sheet for 5 minutes before removing them to wire racks to cool completely.

Black and White "Pretzels"

Children will love these twisty, delicious cookies.

Makes 2$\frac{1}{2}$ to 3 dozen "pretzels"

1 cup unsalted butter, at room temperature
1 cup confectioners' sugar
1 egg
1 teaspoon vanilla
1$\frac{1}{2}$ cups flour
8 ounces semisweet chocolate
2 tablespoons unsalted butter

1. In a medium mixing bowl, cream 1 cup butter and the sugar. Add the egg and vanilla. Mix in the flour. Spoon the dough onto wax paper or plastic wrap and wrap well. Refrigerate 2 hours, or until the dough is stiff.

2. Preheat oven to 375°F. Lightly grease two baking sheets.

3. Remove a third of the dough, keeping the rest refrigerated until you need it. Flour your hands and pinch off a small ball of dough. Using the palms of your hands, roll the ball into a thin rope approximately 8 inches long and $\frac{1}{4}$ inch thick. Form the rope into the shape of a pretzel; repeat with remaining dough and place the pretzel shapes 1 inch apart on the baking sheets. Bake 12 to 15 minutes, or until lightly browned. Remove to wire racks to cool completely.

4. Melt the chocolate and 2 tablespoons butter in a double boiler, stirring until smooth. Cover a baking sheet with wax paper or foil. Dip half of each pretzel in the chocolate and place on the baking sheet to set. To speed the process, refrigerate the cookies until the chocolate is set.

Pecan Crescents

A traditional Christmas treat for many families, these tender
butter cookies can be enjoyed year-round.

Makes about 4 dozen cookies

1 cup butter, softened
$1/4$ cup confectioners' sugar
1 tablespoon water
1 teaspoon vanilla

2 cups flour
2 cups very finely chopped pecans
confectioners' sugar for coating

1. Preheat oven to 325°F. Do not grease baking sheets.

2. In a large bowl, beat the butter until fluffy and white. Gradually
add $1/4$ cup sugar, then beat in water and vanilla until fluffy.
By hand, stir in the flour and pecans. Cover and chill for at least
1 hour. (The dough will be a little sticky.)

3. Using about 1 tablespoon of dough for each cookie, form small
logs, each about 3 inches long. Bend each log into a crescent shape.
Place on ungreased baking sheets and bake 20 minutes, or until
very lightly browned.

4. Put some confectioners' sugar in a bowl, and roll the hot cookies
in it. Place on wire racks to cool completely.

VARIATION: To make smaller cookies, use about 1 teaspoon of
dough to form 1-inch crescents. Bake for about 15 minutes.
Making them this size yields about 12 dozen.

Mexican Chocolate Sugar Cookies

Crisp and sugary on the outside and chewy on the inside, these chocolate treats have a pleasing hint of cinnamon. They are quite hardy, and mail well!

Makes about 4 dozen cookies

1 cup sugar
3/4 cup shortening
1 egg
1/4 cup light corn syrup
2 ounces unsweetened
  chocolate, melted and cooled
  to room temperature

1 3/4 cups flour
2 teaspoons baking soda
1 teaspoon cinnamon
1/4 teaspoon salt
1 cup chocolate chips
1/4 cup sugar, for coating

1. Preheat oven to 350°F. Lightly grease two baking sheets.

2. In a large bowl, cream together 1 cup sugar, shortening, and egg. Stir in the corn syrup and melted chocolate.

3. In a small bowl, mix together the flour, baking soda, cinnamon, and salt. Stir the dry ingredients into the shortening mixture to make a stiff dough. Add chocolate chips and mix to incorporate.

4. Pour 1/4 cup sugar into a shallow bowl or onto a saucer.

5. Shape the dough into 1-inch balls, and roll each ball in sugar. Place on prepared baking sheets, 2 inches apart, and bake 8 to10 minutes, or until the cookies are puffed and the tops crack. Let cookies cool for a few minutes before removing to wire racks to cool completely.

✤ RECIPE:

✤ From the kitchen of:

✤ Yield: _____   ✤ Preheat oven: _____

✤ Ingredients: _____

✤ Directions:

✤ Special notes:

✻ RECIPE:

✻ From the kitchen of:

✻ Yield: _____   ✻ Preheat oven: _____

✻ Ingredients: _____

✻ Directions: _____

✻ Special notes: _____

✤ Recipe:

✤ From the kitchen of:

✤ Yield: ✤ Preheat oven:

✤ Ingredients:

✤ Directions:

✤ Special notes:

❋ RECIPE:

❋ From the kitchen of:

❋ Yield: _____ ❋ Preheat oven: _____

❋ Ingredients: _____

❋ Directions: _____

❋ Special notes: _____

❋ RECIPE: _____

❋ From the kitchen of: _____

❋ Yield: _____   ❋ Preheat oven: _____

❋ Ingredients: _____

_____   _____

_____   _____

_____   _____

_____   _____

_____   _____

❋ Directions: _____

_____

_____

_____

_____

_____

_____

_____

_____

_____

_____

_____

_____

_____

❋ Special notes: _____

_____

_____

_____

✳ RECIPE: _____

✳ From the kitchen of: _____

✳ Yield: _____   ✳ Preheat oven: _____

✳ Ingredients: _____

_____   _____

_____   _____

_____   _____

_____   _____

✳ Directions: _____

_____

_____

_____

_____

_____

_____

_____

_____

_____

_____

_____

_____

✳ Special notes: _____

_____

_____

Strawberry Crumble Bars

Glazed Lemon Bars

Raspberry Coconut Bars

Pecan Wedges

Strawberry Crumble Bars

Bright red strawberry preserves give these bar cookies a festive look. They make a perfect treat for afternoon teas and parties.

Makes 16 (2¼-inch) bars

Crust:
¾ cup unsalted butter, at
   room temperature
½ cup confectioners' sugar
1½ cups flour

Topping:
1 cup flour
1½ cups sugar
1½ cup cold butter, cut into pieces
3 cups flaked coconut
¾ cup strawberry preserves

1. Preheat oven to 350°F. Line a 9-inch square pan with foil; spray the foil with cooking spray.

2. In a medium mixing bowl, with a pastry blender or fork, blend the crust ingredients just until a smooth dough is formed. Press the dough evenly into the bottom of the prepared pan. Bake 15 to 18 minutes, or until the edges begin to brown.

3. While the crust is baking, prepare the crumble: in a medium mixing bowl, stir together the flour and sugar. With a pastry blender or two knives, cut in the butter until mixture is crumbly. Toss in the coconut and mix well.

4. Remove the crust from the oven. Spread the preserves over the hot crust. Sprinkle the crumble evenly over the preserves. Press down lightly. Bake 35 to 45 minutes, or until coconut has browned. Cool completely and cut into bars.

Glazed Lemon Bars

These classic tart lemon squares are an enduring favorite.

Makes 16 (2 1/4-inch) bars

Pastry:
1 1/2 cups flour
3/4 cup unsalted butter, at
  room temperature
1/2 cup sifted confectioners' sugar

Filling:
2 eggs plus 1 egg yolk
1 cup granulated sugar

3 tablespoons fresh lemon juice
grated zest of 1 lemon

Glaze:
1 cup sifted confectioners' sugar
2 teaspoons fresh lemon juice
water as needed

1. Preheat oven to 350°F. Grease a 9-inch square pan.

2. In a medium mixing bowl, combine all the pastry ingredients and mix only until a smooth dough forms. Press dough into bottom of the prepared pan. Bake 15 to 18 minutes, or until the edges are lightly browned.

3. Meanwhile, in a medium mixing bowl, whisk together the ingredients for the filling. Remove the crust from the oven and pour filling evenly over the crust. Bake 25 to 30 minutes, or until the filling is set and begins to brown. Cool for 20 minutes.

4. In a small bowl, beat together the confectioners' sugar and 2 teaspoons lemon juice. Add enough water, 1 teaspoon at a time, to make a spreadable glaze. Spoon the glaze over the filling, covering entirely. Cool completely before cutting into bars.

VARIATION: Before the icing sets, place a candied violet in the center of each bar, pressing down slightly so the flowers stick to the glaze.

Raspberry Coconut Bars

These tasty, tender bars make a great after–school treat
for kids and parents alike.

Makes 16 (2 ¹/₄-inch) bars

Crust:
¹/₂ cup unsalted butter, at
  room temperature
¹/₂ cup granulated sugar
1¹/₂ cups flour

Topping:
²/₃ cup light brown sugar,
  packed

¹/₂ cup flour
6 tablespoons cold unsalted butter
1 cup flaked coconut
¹/₂ cup coarsely chopped pecans
¹/₂ cup mini chocolate chips
³/₄ cup raspberry preserves

1. Preheat oven to 375°F. Line a 9–inch square pan with foil; spray the foil with cooking spray.

2. In a medium mixing bowl, cream the butter and sugar; add the flour and mix until thoroughly combined. Press the dough firmly into the prepared pan. Bake 20 minutes, or until crust begins to brown.

3. While the dough is baking, prepare the topping: in a small mixing bowl, stir together the sugar and flour. With a pastry blender or two knives, cut the butter into the sugar and flour until crumbly. Toss in the coconut, pecans, and chocolate chips; mix well.

4. Remove the dough from the oven. Carefully spread the preserves over the crust. Sprinkle the topping mixture over the preserves, distributing evenly. Press down firmly and return the pan to the oven for an additional 30 minutes, or until the top is browned and firm. Cool completely before cutting into bars.

Pecan Wedges

Rich and nutty, these delicious pecan wedges are even tastier
when dipped in chocolate.

Makes 26 (4¹/₂- by 1-inch) bars

Crust:
- ³/₄ cup unsalted butter, at room temperature
- ¹/₄ cup shortening
- ³/₄ cup confectioners' sugar
- 2 cups flour

Pecan praline:
- 1 cup dark brown sugar, packed
- 1 egg
- 1¹/₂ tablespoons flour
- 1 tablespoon vanilla
- 2 cups pecans, roughly chopped
- 8 ounces good quality milk, semi-sweet, or bittersweet chocolate

1. Preheat oven to 375°F. Line a 9–by–13–inch pan with foil; spray with cooking spray.

2. In a medium mixing bowl, cream together the butter, shortening, and sugar. Beat in the flour, mixing until ingredients are thoroughly combined and a dough forms. Press the dough into the bottom and 1 inch up the sides of the prepared pan. Bake 10 minutes.

3. While the crust is baking, prepare the praline: in a medium mixing bowl, beat together the brown sugar, egg, flour, and vanilla. Mix in the pecans and stir until all the nuts are coated. Remove the crust from the oven and pour the pecan praline over the crust, spreading evenly, leaving 1 inch around the edge of the crust uncovered. Bake 20 minutes, or until the praline has set and the crust has browned. Remove from the oven and cool completely.

4. Melt the chocolate in a double boiler. Pour it into a shallow bowl and set aside. With a sharp knife, cut the praline in half lengthwise, then cut horizontally into 1–inch strips, so you have 26 bars, each with a section of crust on one end. Carefully dip each bar, crust side down, into the melted chocolate. Place each bar on wax paper or foil and allow chocolate to set for at least 1 hour before serving.

❖ RECIPE:

❖ From the kitchen of:

❖ Yield: _____   ❖ Preheat oven: _____

❖ Ingredients:

❖ Directions:

❖ Special notes:

✴ RECIPE:

✴ From the kitchen of:

✴ Yield: _____   ✴ Preheat oven:

✴ Ingredients:

✴ Directions:

✴ Special notes:

✤ RECIPE:

✤ From the kitchen of:

✤ Yield: _____ ✤ Preheat oven: _____

✤ Ingredients: _____

_____ _____

_____ _____

_____ _____

_____ _____

_____ _____

✤ Directions: _____

_____

_____

_____

_____

_____

_____

_____

_____

_____

_____

_____

_____

_____

✤ Special notes: _____

_____

_____

✼ RECIPE:

✼ From the kitchen of: _____

✼ Yield: _____   ✼ Preheat oven: _____

✼ Ingredients: _____

_____

_____

_____

_____

_____

✼ Directions: _____

_____

_____

_____

_____

_____

_____

_____

_____

_____

_____

_____

_____

_____

✼ Special notes: _____

_____

_____

_____

�֎ RECIPE:

✤ From the kitchen of: _____

✤ Yield: _____   ✤ Preheat oven: _____

✤ Ingredients: _____   _____

_____   _____

_____   _____

_____   _____

_____   _____

✤ Directions: _____

_____

_____

_____

_____

_____

_____

_____

_____

_____

_____

_____

_____

_____

✤ Special notes: _____

_____

_____

_____

✳ RECIPE: _____

✳ From the kitchen of: _____

✳ Yield: _____   ✳ Preheat oven: _____

✳ Ingredients: _____   _____
_____   _____
_____   _____
_____   _____
_____   _____
_____   _____

✳ Directions: _____
_____
_____
_____
_____
_____
_____
_____
_____
_____
_____
_____
_____
_____

✳ Special notes: _____
_____
_____
_____

Gingerbread House

Dark Gingerbread

Makes 2 dozen cookies or 1 gingerbread house (see Gingerbread House for instructions)

3³/₄ cups self-rising flour
2 teaspoons ground ginger
¹/₂ teaspoon ground cloves
¹/₂ cup cold unsalted butter

²/₃ cup dark brown sugar
¹/₃ cup molasses
1 egg

1. Preheat oven to 400°F and grease two baking sheets.

2. Put the flour and spices in a food processor. Cut the butter into small pieces, add it to the processor and pulse until the mixture resembles breadcrumbs. Or, in a large mixing bowl, stir together the flour and spices; with a pastry blender or two knives, cut the butter into the flour until the mixture resembles coarse breadcrumbs. Add the sugar, molasses, and egg, and mix well. Wrap the dough in wax paper or plastic wrap and chill for at least 30 minutes.

3. Roll out the mixture on a floured surface. Cut out rounds or squares and place on the baking sheets. Bake for 12 to 15 minutes until the shapes have risen slightly and appear a little paler in color. Leave on the baking sheets for 2 minutes, then transfer to wire racks to cool.

Gingerbread House Templates

Enlarge templates by 200 percent

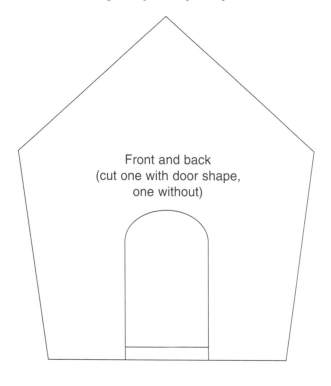

Front and back
(cut one with door shape,
one without)

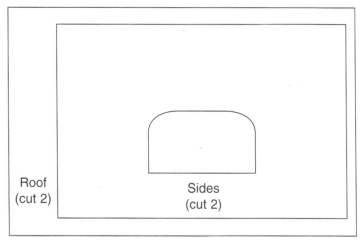

Roof
(cut 2)

Sides
(cut 2)

Gingerbread House

Often associated with fairy-tale characters Hansel and Gretel, a gingerbread house makes a cheerful and tasty centerpiece for a winter birthday or Christmas party.

Makes 1 gingerbread house

Special equipment:
paper for templates (see separate recipe page)
scissors
1¹/₂-inch round cookie cutter
sharp paring knife
an 11 × 8-inch rectangle of sturdy cardboard covered with foil
plastic sandwich bag

dark gingerbread dough (see separate recipe page)

Icing and decoration:
4 quantities royal icing (see introduction)
10 small ratafia cookies or ginger snaps
15 to 18 small chocolate truffles or peppermint patties
3 ounces chocolate-covered raisins
7 small wafer-thin chocolate cookies
small packet candy-covered chocolates
1 chocolate-covered nougat candy bar, thinly sliced

1. Preheat the oven to 400°F and grease two baking sheets.

2. Enlarge the gingerbread house templates by 200 percent on a photocopier and cut them out with scissors. Roll out the gingerbread dough and with a sharp paring knife, cut out the cottage shapes. Use the template to cut a door for the cottage front and then trim ¹/₄ inch off the base of the door. Cut out windows from the cottage sides. Using a small round cutter, cut out a window from the area above the door.

3. Transfer all the pieces, including the door, to the baking sheets and bake for about 15 minutes until slightly risen. Leave the pieces on the tray for 2 minutes before transferring them to a wire cooling rack.

4. Spread royal icing along the base and up the sides of one side wall section. Spread more icing along the base of the front wall and secure the two sections together on the cardboard, propping the pieces up with small drinking glasses until they are firmly set. Secure the back wall, then the other side, and allow to set for about 30 minutes.

5. If the icing feels stiff and won't spread easily, thin with a little water. Spread icing over the top edges of the side walls and secure one of the roof sections, again using drinking glasses to give the shapes support. Spread icing along the top of the roof and secure the other piece in place. Using a palette knife or a narrow metal spatula, spread a thin layer of icing over the roof.

6. To form icicles, hold a teaspoon of icing at an angle above the edges of the roof. As the icing starts to slip from the spoon, catch it along the edges, to create the impression of dangling icicles. (Again, if the icing is too stiff, thin it with a little water.)

7. Use the ratafia cookies or ginger snaps, chocolate truffles or peppermint patties, and chocolate-covered raisins to decorate the roof. Add a single row of chocolate-covered raisins along the top of the roof. If they don't stick, secure with small amounts of icing.

8. Spoon a little icing into a small plastic sandwich bag; set aside. Spread the remaining icing over the board to make "snow."

9. With scissors, cut a tiny opening in a corner of the plastic sand-wich bag and pipe a little icing onto the backs of the wafer-thin chocolate cookies and secure them on both sides of the windows. Arrange the remaining cookies at the front of the cottage, to create the impression of steps.

10. Pipe a line of icing around the door and press the door in position. Decorate the window ledges and the small round window with chocolate-covered raisins, securing each into position with a dab of icing. Secure another raisin for the doorknob and place a few candy-covered chocolates on the iced board to suggest a path.

11. Use the icing in the bag to pipe decorative edges around the door and along the corners of the cottage. Add slices of the chocolate-covered nougat candy bar around the base.

TIP

For an extra surprise, fill the house with candy and cookies before placing the roof in position.

From *Decorating Cookies* by Joanna Farrow. Copyright ©2000 Merehurst Limited, First published in the United States of America in 2001 by Watson-Guptill Publications, New York. www.watsonguptill.com

✢ RECIPE:

✢ From the kitchen of:

✢ Yield: _____   ✢ Preheat oven: _____

✢ Ingredients: _____

✢ Directions: _____

✢ Special notes: _____

✽ RECIPE: _____

✽ From the kitchen of: _____

✽ Yield: _____   ✽ Preheat oven: _____

✽ Ingredients: _____   _____

_____   _____

_____   _____

_____   _____

_____   _____

✽ Directions: _____

_____

_____

_____

_____

_____

_____

_____

_____

_____

_____

_____

_____

_____

✽ Special notes: _____

_____

_____

❊ RECIPE: _____

❊ From the kitchen of: _____

❊ Yield: _____   ❊ Preheat oven: _____

❊ Ingredients: _____   _____

_____   _____

_____   _____

_____   _____

_____   _____

_____   _____

❊ Directions: _____

_____

_____

_____

_____

_____

_____

_____

_____

_____

_____

_____

_____

_____

❊ Special notes: _____

_____

_____

_____

✠ RECIPE:

✠ From the kitchen of:

✠ Yield: _____   ✠ Preheat oven: _____

✠ Ingredients: _____   _____

✠ Directions:

✠ Special notes:

❈ RECIPE: _____

❈ From the kitchen of: _____

❈ Yield: _____   ❈ Preheat oven: _____

❈ Ingredients: _____   _____

_____   _____

_____   _____

_____   _____

_____   _____

❈ Directions: _____

_____

_____

_____

_____

_____

_____

_____

_____

_____

_____

_____

_____

_____

❈ Special notes: _____

_____

_____

_____

✻ RECIPE: _____

✻ From the kitchen of: _____

✻ Yield: _____   ✻ Preheat oven: _____

✻ Ingredients: _____   _____

_____   _____

_____   _____

_____   _____

_____   _____

✻ Directions: _____

_____

_____

_____

_____

_____

_____

_____

_____

_____

_____

_____

_____

_____

✻ Special notes: _____

_____

_____

_____